CW00833737

My I

St Pa

MY

NAME

IS PATRICK

ST PATRICK'S *CONFESSIO*

Translated by Pádraig McCarthy

ROYAL IRISH ACADEMY

My name is Patrick: St Patrick's *Confessio*

First published 2011

by Royal Irish Academy
19 Dawson Street
Dublin 2

www.ria.ie

The text is a translation from the Latin by Pádraig McCarthy,
Sandyford, Dublin 16, Ireland. © 2008

ISBN 978-1-904890-84-3

The St Patrick's Confessio Hypertext Stack is constructed under the
auspices of the Royal Irish Academy's Dictionary of Medieval Latin
from Celtic Sources (DMLCS) project.

The RIA is grateful to the following for supporting this publication
and the Hypertext Stack:

 Ireland's EU Structural Funds
Programmes 2007 · 2013

Co-funded by the Irish Government
and the European Union

 EUROPEAN REGIONAL
DEVELOPMENT FUND

 An Roinn Post, Fiontar agus Nuálaíochta
Department of Jobs, Enterprise and Innovation

 HEA
Higher Education Authority
An tÚdarás um Ard-Oideachas

British Library Cataloguing in Publication Data. A CIP catalogue
record for this book is available from the British Library.

Printed in Ireland by Walsh Colour Print

10 9 8 7 6 5 4 3 2 1

I.

My name is Patrick. I am a sinner, a simple country person, and the least of all believers. I am looked down upon by many.

My father was Calpornius. He was a deacon; his father was Potitus, a priest, who lived at Bannavem Taburniae.[1] His home was near there, and that is where I was taken prisoner. I was about sixteen at the time.

At that time, I did not know the true God. I was taken into captivity in Ireland, along with thousands of others. We deserved this, because we had gone away from God, and did not keep his commandments. We would not listen to our priests, who advised us about how we could be saved.[2] The Lord brought his strong anger upon us, and scattered us among many nations even to the ends of the earth. It was among foreigners that it was seen how little I was.

2.

It was there that the Lord opened up my awareness of my lack of faith. Even though it came about late, I recognised my failings. So I turned with all my heart to the Lord my God,[3] and he looked down on my lowliness[4] and had mercy on my youthful ignorance. He guarded me before I knew him, and before I came to wisdom and could distinguish between good and evil. He protected me and consoled me as a father does for his son.

3·

That is why I cannot be silent—nor would it be good to do so—about such great blessings and such a gift that the Lord so kindly bestowed in the land of my captivity. This is how we can repay such blessings, when our lives change and we come to know God, to praise and bear witness to his great wonders before every nation under heaven.

4·

This is because there is no other God, nor will there ever be, nor was there ever, except God the Father. He is the one who was not begotten, the one without a beginning, the one from whom all beginnings come, the one who holds all things in being—this is our teaching.

And his son, Jesus Christ, whom we testify has always been, since before the beginning of this age, with the father in a spiritual way. He was begotten in an indescribable way before every beginning. Everything we can see, and everything beyond our sight, was made through him. He became a human being; and, having overcome death, was welcomed to the heavens to the Father. The Father gave him all power over every being, both heavenly and earthly and beneath the earth. Let every tongue confess that Jesus Christ, in whom we believe and whom we await to come back to us in the near future, is Lord and God.[5] He is judge of the living and of the dead;[6] he rewards every person according to their deeds.[7] He has generously poured on us the Holy Spirit,[8] the gift and promise of immortality, who makes believers and those who listen to be children of God and co-heirs with Christ.[9] This is the one we acknowledge and adore—one God in a trinity of the sacred name.

5.

He said through the prophet: 'Call on me in the day of your distress, and I will set you free, and you will glorify me'.[10] Again he said: 'It is a matter of honour to reveal and tell forth the works of God'.[11]

6.

Although I am imperfect in many ways, I want my brothers and relations to know what I'm really like, so that they can see what it is that inspires my life.

7.

I am not ignoring the evidence of my Lord, who testifies in the psalm: 'You destroy those who speak lies'.[12] And again he says: 'A mouth which lies kills the soul'. And the same Lord says in the gospel: 'The idle words which people speak, they will account for on the day of judgment'.[13]

8.

So I should greatly dread, with fear and trembling, this sentence on that day, where nobody can avoid or escape, but all shall give complete account of the least of sins before the tribunal of the Lord Christ.

9.

This is why I have long thought to write, but up to now I have hesitated, because I feared what people would say. This is because I did not learn as others did, who drank in equally well both the law and the sacred writings, and never had to change their way of speaking since childhood, but always grew better and better at it. For me, however, my speech and words have been translated into a foreign language, as it can be easily seen from my writings the standard of the instruction and learning I have had. As it is said: 'The wise person is known through speech, and also understanding and knowledge and the teaching of truth'.[14]

10.

However, even though there's truth in my excuse, it gets me nowhere. Now, in my old age, I want to do what I was unable to do in my youth. My sins then prevented me from really taking in what I read. But who believes me, even were I to repeat what I said previously? I was taken prisoner as a youth, particularly young in the matter of being able to speak, and before I knew what I should seek and what I should avoid. That is why, today, I blush and am afraid to expose my lack of experience, because I can't express myself with the brief words I would like in my heart and soul.

11.

If I had been given the same chance as other people, I would not be silent, whatever the reward. If I seem to some to be too forward, with my lack of knowledge and my even slower tongue, still it is written: 'Stammering tongues will quickly learn to speak peace'.[15] How much more should we want to do this, who are, as it is said, a saving letter of Christ even to the ends of the earth. Although it is not well expressed, still this letter is genuinely and strongly written in your hearts, not with ink, but with the spirit of the living God.[16] The Spirit is a witness that what is of the country-side is also created by the Most High!

12.

So I am first of all a simple country person, a refugee, and unlearned. I do not know how to provide for the future. But this I know for certain, that before I was brought low, I was like a stone lying deep in the mud. Then he who is powerful came and in his mercy pulled me out, and lifted me up and placed me on the very top of the wall.[17] That is why I must shout aloud in return to the Lord for such great good deeds of his, here and now and forever, which the human mind cannot measure.

13.

So be amazed, all you people great and small who fear God! You well-educated people in authority, listen and examine this carefully.

Who was it who called one as foolish as I am[18] from the middle of those who are seen to be wise and experienced in law and powerful in speech and in everything? If I am most looked down upon, yet he inspired me, before others, so that I would faithfully serve the nations with awe and reverence and without blame: the nations to whom the love of Christ brought me.[19] His gift was that I would spend my life, if I were worthy of it, serving them in truth and with humility to the end.

14.

In the knowledge of this faith in the Trinity, and without letting the dangers prevent it, it is right to make known the gift of God and his eternal consolation. It is right to spread abroad the name of God faithfully and without fear, so that even after my death I may leave something of value to the many thousands of my brothers and sisters—the children whom I baptised in the Lord.

15.

I didn't deserve at all that the Lord would grant such great grace, after hardships and troubles, after captivity, and after so many years among that people. It was something which, when I was young, I never hoped for or even thought of.

16.

After I arrived in Ireland, I tended sheep every day, and I prayed frequently during the day. More and more the love of God increased, and my sense of awe before God. Faith grew, and my spirit was moved, so that in one day I would pray up to one hundred times, and at night perhaps the same. I even remained in the woods and on the mountain, and I would rise to pray before dawn in snow and ice and rain. I never felt the worse for it, and I never felt lazy—as I realise now, the spirit was burning in me at that time.

17.

It was there one night in my sleep that I heard a voice saying to me: 'You have fasted well. Very soon you will return to your native country.' Again after a short while, I heard a someone saying to me: 'Look—your ship is ready'. It was not nearby, but a good two hundred miles away. I had never been to the place, nor did I know anyone there. So I ran away then, and left the man with whom I had been for six years. It was in the strength of God that I went—God who turned the direction of my life to good; I feared nothing while I was on the journey to that ship.

18.

The day I arrived, the ship was about to leave the place. I said I needed to set sail with them, but the captain was not at all pleased. He replied unpleasantly and angrily: 'Don't you dare try to come with us'. When I heard that, I left them and went back to the hut where I had lodgings. I began to pray while I was going; and before I even finished the prayer, I heard one of them shout aloud at me: 'Come quickly—those men are calling you!' I turned back right away, and they began to say to me: 'Come—we'll trust you. Prove you're our friend in any way you wish'. That day, I refused to suck their breasts, because of my reverence for God.[20] They were pagans, and I hoped they might come to faith in Jesus Christ. This is how I got to go with them, and we set sail right away.

19.

After three days we made it to land, and then for twenty-eight days we travelled through a wilderness. Food ran out, and great hunger came over them. The captain turned to me and said: 'What about this, Christian? You tell us that your God is great and all-powerful—why can't you pray for us, since we're in a bad state with hunger? There's no sign of us finding a human being anywhere!' Then I said to them with some confidence: 'Turn in faith with all your hearts to the Lord my God,[21] because nothing is impossible for him,[22] so that he may put food in your way—even enough to make you fully satisfied! He has an abundance everywhere'. With the help of God, this is actually what happened! A herd of pigs appeared in the way before our eyes! They killed many of them and there they remained for two nights, and were fully restored, and the dogs too were filled. Many of them had grown weak and left half-alive by the way. After this, they gave the greatest of thanks to God, and I was honoured in their eyes. From this day on, they had plenty of food. They also found some wild honey, and offered some of it to me. However, one of them said: 'This honey must have been offered in sacrifice to a god'. Thanks be to God, from then on I tasted none of it.

20.

That same night while I was sleeping, Satan strongly put me to the test—I will remember it as long as I live! It was as if an enormous rock fell on me, and I lost all power in my limbs.

Although I knew little about the life of the spirit at the time, how was it that I knew to call upon Helias?[23] While these things were happening, I saw the sun rise in the sky, and while I was calling 'Helias! Helias!' with all my strength, the splendour of the sun fell on me; and immediately, all that weight was lifted from me. I believe that I was helped by Christ the Lord, and that his spirit cried out for me. I trust that it will be like this whenever I am under stress, as the gospel says: 'In that day, the Lord testifies, it will not be you will speak, but the Spirit of your Father who speaks in you'.[24]

21.

It happened again after many years that I was taken a prisoner. On the first night I was with them, I heard a divine answer saying to me: 'You will be with them for two months'. This is how it was: on the sixtieth night, the Lord freed me from their hands.

22.*

While we were still on the journey, the Lord provided food and fire and shelter every day until we met some people on the tenth day. As I mentioned above, we travelled for twenty-

* This section would seem to fit in more suitably after paragraph 19. It seems possible that section 22 somehow slipped out of place at some stage. Perhaps it was a mistake made in copying by a scribe.

eight days through the wilderness. On the very night we met people, we ran out of food.

23.

A few years later I was again with my parents in Britain. They welcomed me as a son, and they pleaded with me that, after all the many tribulations I had undergone, I should never leave them again. It was while I was there that I saw, in a vision in the night, a man[25] whose name was Victoricus coming as it were from Ireland with so many letters they could not be counted. He gave me one of these, and I read the beginning of the letter, the voice of the Irish people. While I was reading out the beginning of the letter, I thought I heard at that moment the voice of those who were beside the wood of Voclut, near the western sea.[26] They called out as it were with one voice: 'We beg you, holy boy, to come and walk again among us'. This touched my heart deeply, and I could not read any further; I woke up then. Thanks be to God, after many years the Lord granted them what they were calling for.

24.

Another night—I do not know, God knows, whether it was within me or beside me[27]—I heard authoritative words which I could hear but not understand, until at the end of the speech it became clear: 'The one who gave his life for you, he it is who speaks in you'; and I awoke full of joy.

25.

Another time, I saw in me one who was praying. It was as if I were inside my body, and I heard above me, that is, above my inner self. He prayed strongly, with sighs. I was amazed and astonished, and pondered who it was who prayed in me; but at the end of the prayer, it was clear that it was the Spirit. At this I awoke, and I remembered the apostle saying: 'The Spirit helps the weaknesses of our prayer; for we do know what it is we should pray, but the very Spirit pleads for us with unspeakable sighs, which cannot be expressed in words'.[28] And again: 'The Lord is our advocate, and pleads for us'.[29]

26.

One time I was put to the test by some superiors of mine. They came and put my sins against my hard work as a bishop. This hit me very hard, so much so that it seemed I was about to fall, both here and in eternity. But

the Lord in his kindness spared the converts
and the strangers for the sake of his name,
and strongly supported me when I was so
badly treated. I did not slip into sin and disgrace. I pray that God not hold this sin
against them.[30]

27.

They brought up against me after 30 years
something I had already confessed before I was
a deacon. What happened was that, one day
when I was feeling anxious and low, with a
very dear friend of mine I referred to some
things I had done one day—rather, in one
hour—when I was young, before I overcame
my weakness. I don't know—God knows—
whether I was then fifteen years old at the
time, and I did not then believe in the living
God, not even when I was a child. In fact, I remained in death and unbelief until I was
reproved strongly, and actually brought low by
hunger and nakedness daily.

28.

My defence was that I remained on in Ireland,
and that not of my own choosing, until I
almost perished. However, it was very good for
me, since God straightened me out, and he

prepared me for what I would be today. I was far different then from what I am now, and I have care for others, and I have enough to do to save them. In those days I did not even have concern for my own welfare.

29.

So on the day I was accused by those I mentioned above, that same night I saw in a vision of the night some writing before my dishonoured face. In the middle of this, I heard an answer from God saying to me: 'We have seen with displeasure the face of the one who was chosen deprived of his good name'. He did not say: 'You have seen with displeasure', but 'We have seen with displeasure', as if he were identifying himself with me; as he said 'He who touches you as it were touches the pupil of my eye'.[31]

30.

For that reason, I give thanks to the one who strengthened me in all things,[32] so that he would not impede me in the course I had undertaken and from the works also which I had learned from Christ my Lord. Rather, I sensed in myself no little strength from him, and my faith passed the test before God and people.

31.

I make bold to say that my conscience does not blame me, now and in the future.[33] I have God for witness that I have not told lies in the account I have given you.

32.

But I grieve more for my very dear friend, that we had to hear such an account—the one to whom I entrusted my very soul. I did learn from some brothers before the case was heard that he came to my defence in my absence. I was not there at the time, not even in Britain, and it was not I who brought up the matter. In fact it was he himself who told me from his own mouth: 'Look, you are being given the rank of bishop'. That is something I did not deserve. How could he then afterwards come to disgrace me in public before all, both good and bad, about a matter for which he had already freely and joyfully forgiven me, as indeed had God, who is greater than all?

33.

I have said enough about that. I must take care not to hide the gift of God which he has generously given us in the land of my captivity. It was then that I looked for him with all my strength, and there I found him, and he protected me from all evils—this is what I believe—on account of his Spirit living and working in me to this very day. I'm proud to tell again of this. God knows, if it were some other person who had said this to me, perhaps I would have said nothing, because of the love of Christ.

34.

So I'll never stop giving thanks to my God, who kept me faithful in the time of my temptation. I can today with confidence offer my soul to Christ my Lord as a living victim.[34] He is the one who defended me in all my difficulties. I can say: 'Who am I, Lord, or what is my calling, that you have worked with me with such divine presence?'[35] This is how I come to praise and magnify your name among the nations all the time, wherever I am, not only in good times but in the difficult times too. Whatever comes about for me, good or bad, I ought to accept them equally and give thanks to God. He has shown me that I can put my faith in him without wavering and without end. However ignorant I am, he has heard me, so that in these late days I can dare to undertake such a holy and wonderful work. In this way I can imitate somewhat those whom the Lord foretold would announce his gospel in witness to all nations before the end of the world. This is what we see has been fulfilled. Look at us: we are witnesses that the gospel has been preached right out to where there is nobody else there!

35.

It's a long story—to tell each and every deed of mine, or even parts of it. I'll make it short, as I tell of how the good God often freed me from slavery, and from twelve dangers which threatened my life, as well as from hidden dangers and from things which I have no words to express. I wouldn't want to hurt my readers! God knows all things even before they are done, and I have him as my authority that he often gave me warnings in heavenly answers,—me, a wretched orphan!

36.

From where did this wisdom come to me, a wisdom which was not in me?[36] I didn't even know how the number of my days,[37] much less did I know God. Where did such a great and life-giving gift come from then, to know and love God, even at the cost of leaving homeland and parents?

37.

And many were the gifts offered to me, along with sorrow and tears. There were those whom I offended, even against the wishes of some of my superiors; but, with God guiding me, I did not consent nor acquiesce to them. It was not by my own grace, but God who overcame it in me, and resisted them all so that I could come to the peoples of Ireland to preach the gospel. I bore insults from unbelievers, so that I would hear the hatred directed at me for travelling here. I bore many persecutions, even chains, so that I could give up my freeborn state for the sake of others. If I be worthy, I am ready even to give up my life most willingly here and now for his name. It is there that I wish to spend my life until I die, if the Lord should grant it to me.

38.

I am greatly in debt to God. He gave me such great grace, that through me, many people should be born again in God and brought to full life. Also that clerics should be ordained everywhere for this people who have lately come to believe, and who the Lord has taken from the ends of the earth. This is just what he promised in the past through his prophet: 'The nations will come to you from the ends of the earth, and they will say: How false are the idols our fathers got for themselves, and they are of no use whatever'.[38] And again: 'I have put you as a light to the nations, that you may be their salvation to the end of the earth'.[39]

39.

It is there that I await his promise—he is the one who never deceives, as is repeated in the gospel: 'They will come from the east and from the west, and they will lie down with Abraham and Isaac and Jacob'.[40] We believe that believing people will come from all over the world.

40.

It is right that we should fish well and diligently, as the Lord directs and teaches when he says: 'Follow me, and I will make you fishers of men'.[41] And again he says through the prophets: 'Behold, I send many fishers and hunters, says God';[42] and other such sayings. Therefore it is very right that we should cast our nets, so that a great multitude and crowd will be taken for God. Also that there should be clerics to baptise and encourage a people in need and want. This is what the Lord says in the gospel: he warns and teaches in these words: 'Go therefore and teach all nations, baptising them in the name of the Father and of the Son and of the Holy Spirit, teaching them to observe all that I have commanded you; and behold I am with you all days, even to the end of the age'.[43] Again he says: 'Go out therefore to the whole world and announce the gospel to every creature. Whoever believes and is baptised will be saved; whoever does not believe will be condemned'.[44] And yet again: 'This gospel of the kingdom will be announced all over the world, as testimony to all the nations; and then will come the end'.[45] In the same way, the Lord foretold this through the prophet as he said: 'And it will come about in the last days, says the Lord, that I will pour out my Spirit on all flesh, and your sons and your daughters will prophesy; your young people will see visions and your older people will dream dreams. Indeed, on my servants, men and women, I will pour out my Spirit and they will prophesy'.[46] Hosea says: 'Those who were not my people, I will call my people; and her who has not obtained mercy, I will name the one who has obtained mercy.[47] In the place where it was said: You are not my people: there they will be called children of the living God'.[48]

4I.

How has this happened in Ireland? Never before did they know of God except to serve idols and unclean things. But now, they have become the people of the Lord, and are called children of God. The sons and daughters of the leaders of the Irish are seen to be monks and virgins of Christ!

42.

An example is this. There was a blessed Irish woman of noble birth, a most beautiful adult whom I baptised. She came to us a few days later for this reason. She told us that she had received word from a messenger of God, who advised her that she should become a virgin of Christ, and that she should come close to God. Thanks be to God, six days later, enthusiastically and well, she took on the life that all virgins of God do. Their fathers don't like this, of course. These women suffer persecution and false accusations from their parents, and yet their number grows! We do not know the number of our people who were born there. In addition, there are the widows and the celibates. Of all these, those held in slavery work hardest—they bear even terror and threats, but the Lord gives grace to so many of the women who serve him. Even when it is forbidden, they bravely follow his example.

43.

I could wish to leave them to go to Britain. I would willingly do this, and am prepared for this, as if to visit my home country and my parents. Not only that, but I would like to go to Gaul to visit the brothers and to see the faces of the saints of my Lord. God knows what I would dearly like to do. But I am bound in the Spirit, who assures me that if I were to do this, I would be held guilty. And I fear, also, to lose the work which I began—not so much I as Christ the Lord, who told me to come here to be with these people for the rest of my life. May the Lord will it, and protect me from every wrong path, so that I do not sin before him.

44.

I hope to do what I should. I know I cannot trust myself as long as I am in this body subject to death.[49] There is one who is strong, who tries every day to undermine my faith, and the chastity of genuine religion I have chosen to the end of my life for Christ my Lord. The flesh can be an enemy dragging towards death, that is, towards doing those enticing things which are against the law. I know to some extent how I have not led a perfect life like other believers. But I acknowledge this to my Lord, and I do not blush in his sight. I am not telling lies: from the time in my youth that I came to know him, the love and reverence for God grew in me, and so far, with the Lord's help, I have kept faith.

45.

Those who wish may laugh and insult. But I will not be silent, nor will I hide the signs and wonders which the Lord has shown me even many years before they came about. He knows all things even before the beginning of time.

46.

So I want to give thanks to God without ceasing. He frequently forgave my lack of wisdom and my negligence, and more than once did not become very angry with me, the one who was meant to be his helper. I was not quick to accept what he showed me, and so the Spirit prompted me. The Lord was merciful to me a thousand thousand times, because he saw in me that I was ready, but that I did not know what I should do about the state of my life. There were many who forbade this mission.

They even told stories among themselves behind my back, and the said: 'Why does he put himself in danger among hostile people who do not know God?' It was not that they were malicious—they just did not understand, as I myself can testify, since I was just an unlearned country person. Indeed, I was not quick to recognise the grace that was in me; I know now what I should have done then.

47.

Now, therefore, I have informed my brothers and my fellow-servants who believed me, because I gave them warning, and I warn them now, in order to strengthen and confirm your faith. Oh that you would imitate greater things, and do more powerful things![50] This will be my glory, since a wise son is the glory of his father![51]

48.

You all know, and God knows, how I have lived among you since my youth, in true faith and in sincerity of heart. Towards the pagan people too among whom I live, I have lived in good faith, and will continue to do so. God knows that I have not been devious with even one of them, nor do I think of doing so, for the sake of God and his church. I would not want to arouse persecution of them and of all of us; nor would I want that the Lord's name should be blasphemed on account of me; since it is written: 'Woe to the one through whom the name of the Lord is blasphemed'.[52]

49.

I know that I am inexperienced in all things. But still, I have tried to keep a guard on myself and for the Christians and virgins of Christ and religious women who were giving me small gifts of their own accord. When they would throw some of their ornaments on the altar, I would give them back to them. They were hurt at me that I would do this. But it was because of the hope of the eternal gift, that I was careful in all things, in case unbelievers would trap me or my ministry of service for any reason. Nor did I want to give those who could not believe even the slightest reason for speaking against me or to take my character away.

50.

Perhaps, however, when I baptised so many thousands of people, did I hope to receive even the smallest payment? If so, tell me, and I will return it to you. Or when the Lord ordained clerics everywhere through my poor efforts, and I gave this service to them for free, if I asked them to pay even for the cost of my shoes—tell it against me, and I will return it to you and more.

51.

I spend myself for you, so that you may have me for yours. I have travelled everywhere among you for your own sake, in many dangers, and even to the furthest parts where nobody lived beyond, and where nobody ever went to baptise and to ordain clerics or to bring people to fulfilment. It is only by God's gift that I diligently and most willingly did all of this for your good.

52.

At times I gave gifts to kings, over and above what I paid to their sons who travelled with me. Despite this, they took me and my companions prisoner, and very much wanted to kill me, but the time had not yet come. They stole everything they found in our possession, and they bound me in iron. On the fourteenth day, the Lord set me free from their power; all our possessions were returned to us for God's sake, and for the sake of the close friendship we had had previously.

53.

You know yourselves how much I expended on those who were the judges in those regions which I most frequently visited. I estimate that I gave out not less than the price of fifteen persons, so that you might benefit from me, and that I might benefit from you in God. I'm not[53] sorry I did it, nor was it even enough for me— I still spend, and will spend more. The Lord is powerful, and he can grant me still to spend my very self for the sake of your souls.[54]

54.

See now: I call on God as witness in my soul that I tell no lie.[55] Nor would I write to you looking for your praise, nor out of greed—it's not that I hope for honour from any of you for myself. It is the honour which is not yet to be seen, but which is believed in the heart, which is what gives me satisfaction. The one who gave the promise is faithful, and never lies.

55.

I see that already in this present age the Lord has given me a greatness more than could be expected. I was not worthy of this, not the kind of person the Lord would do this for, since I know for certain that poverty and calamity are more my style than riches and enjoyment. But Christ the Lord became poor for us;[56] I too am wretched and unhappy. Even if I were to wish for riches, I do not have them. I am not trying to judge myself, since every day there is the chance that I will be killed, or surrounded, or be taken into slavery, or some other such happening. But I fear none of these things, because of the promises of heaven. I have cast myself into the hands of almighty God, who is the ruler of all places, as the prophet says: 'Cast your concerns on God, and he will sustain you'.[57]

56.

Now I commend my soul to my most faithful God.[58] For him I perform the work of an ambassador,[59] despite my less than noble condition. However, God is not influenced by such personal situations, and he chose me for this task so that I would be one servant of his very least important servants.

57.

So I shall make a return to him for all that he has given to me.[60] But what can I say, or what can I promise to my Lord? There is nothing I have that is not his gift to me. But he knows the depths of my heart, my very gut feelings! He knows that it is enough that I desire very much, and am ready for this, that he would grant me to drink of his chalice, just as he was pleased to do for others who loved him.[61]

58.

For this reason, may God not let it come about that I would suffer the loss of his people who have become his in the furthermost parts of the earth. I pray that God give me perseverance, and that he grant me to bear faithful witness to him right up to my passing from this life, for the sake of my God.

59.

If I have ever imitated anything good for the sake of my God whom I love, I ask that he grant me to be able to shed my blood with these converts and captives—even were I to lack a grave for burial, or my dead body were to be miserably torn apart limb from limb by dogs or wild beasts, or were the birds of heaven to devour it. I declare with certainty that if this were to happen, I would have gained both my soul and my body. There is no doubt whatever that we will rise on the appointed day in the brightness of the sun, that is, in the glory of Christ Jesus our redeemer. We shall be like children of the living God and co-heirs of Christ[62] and to be fashioned in his image, since it is from him and through him and in him that we are to reign.

60.

The sun which we see rising for us each day at his command, that sun will never reign nor will its splendour continue forever; and all those who adore that sun will come to a bad, miserable penalty. We, however, believe in and adore the true sun, that is, Christ, who will never perish. Nor will they perish who do his will but they will abide forever just as Christ will abide forever.[63] He lives with God the Father almighty and with the Holy Spirit before the ages began, and now, and for all the ages of ages. Amen.

61.

Again and again I briefly put before you the words of my confession. I testify in truth and in great joy of heart before God and his holy angels that I never had any other reason for returning to that nation from which I had earlier escaped, except the gospel and God's promises.

62.

I pray for those who believe in and have reverence for God. Some of them may happen to inspect or come upon this writing which Patrick, a sinner without learning, wrote in Ireland. May none of them ever say that whatever little I did or made known to please God was done through ignorance. Instead, you can judge and believe in all truth that it was a gift of God. This is my confession before I die.

NOTES

[1] There are various theories about the whereabouts of Bannavem Taburniae; none is conclusive. In *section 43*, he writes of going to Britain, with the intriguing phrase '*quasi ad patriam*' – 'as though (or nearly) to my native land'. He mentions Britain also in *section 23*.

[2] Daniel 9:5–6: We have gone aside from your commandments…we have not listened to your servants the prophets.

[3] Joel 2:11: Come back to me with all your heart.

[4] Luke 1:48: He looked on the lowliness of his servant.

[5] Philippians 2:9–11: Every knee should bow at the name of Jesus, in heaven, on earth, and under the earth. Every tongue should confess that Jesus Christ is Lord, to the glory of God the Father.

[6] Acts 10:42: God appointed him judge of the living and of the dead.

[7] Romans 2:6: He will reward each one according to his works.

[8] Titus 3:5–6: The Holy Spirit, whom he abundantly poured upon us.

[9] Romans 8:16–17: We are children of God, and joint heirs with Christ.

[10] Psalm 49 (50):15: Call on me in the day of trouble. I will deliver you and you will glorify me.

[11] Tobit 12:7: It is honourable to reveal and confess the works of God.

[12] Psalm 5:7: You destroy all who speak a lie.

[13] Matthew 12:36: Every idle word that people speak, they shall render an account for it on the day of judgement.

[14] Sirach 4:29: Wisdom is recognised through the tongue, and knowledge and learning by the word of the wise.

[15] Isaiah 32:4: The stammering tongue will speak readily and plain.

[16] 2 Corinthians 3:2: You are our letter, written on our hearts, known and read by all.

[17] Psalm 68 (69):15: Draw me out of the mire, so that I may not stick fast.

[18] 1 Corinthians 1:27: God chooses the foolish.

[19] 2 Corinthians 5:14: The love of Christ urges me on.

[20] The practice of symbolically coming under the protection of another by sucking the breast was known in North Africa, Ethiopia, Egypt, Turkey, Armenia, the Caucasus region and Albania, as well as Ireland.

[21] Joel 2:12: Turn to me with all your heart.

[22] Luke 1:37: Nothing is impossible to God.

[23] Significance uncertain: he may be referring to the prophet Elijah (Elias in Latin). Jesus on the cross (Matthew 27:46–47) called on God using the Hebrew name 'Eli', and bystanders thought he was calling on Elijah. Patrick may also be playing with words, as he refers to the sun shining on him – the Greek for 'sun' is Helios. In *section 60*, Patrick writes of the sun again, and says that Jesus Christ is the sun that does not perish.

[24] Matthew 10:19–20: It is not you that speaks, but the Spirit of your Father who speaks in you.

[25] Daniel 7:13: I saw in a vision of the night one like the Son of Man.

[26] Voclut (or Foclut) is unknown.

[27] 2 Corinthians 12:2–3: Whether in the body I know not, or out of the body, I know not; God knows.

[28] Romans 8:26: The Spirit helps our weakness. We do not know what to pray as we ought, but the Spirit pleads within us with unspeakable sighs.

[29] 1 John 2:1: We have an advocate, Jesus Christ, the just one.

[30] Acts 7:60: Lord, do not hold this sin against them.

[31] Zechariah 2:8 (or 2:12): He who touches you touches the apple of my eye

[32] 1 Timothy 1:12: I give thanks to the one who strengthened me.

[33] 1 John 3:21: If our conscience does not condemn us, we can be fearless before God.

[34] Romans 12:1: Offer your bodies as a living sacrifice.

[35] 2 Samuel 7:18: Who am I, Lord, that you have done so much for me?

[36] Matthew 13:54 (Said of Jesus): Where did he get this wisdom?

[37] Job 38:21: Did you know the number of your days?

[38] Jeremiah 16:19: The nations shall come to you from the ends of the earth, and they shall say: Surely our fathers possessed lies, empty things of no profit to them.

[39] Isaiah 49:6: I have made you a light to the nations, so that you may be my salvation to the ends of the earth.

[40] Matthew 8:11: Many will come from the east and the west, and shall sit down with Abraham and Isaac and Jacob.

[41] Matthew 4:19: Follow me, and I will make you fishers of men.

[42] Jeremiah 16:16: Behold, I will send many fishers…after this I will send them many hunters.

[43] Matthew 28:19–20: Going, therefore, teach all nations, baptising them in the name of the Father and of the Son and of the Holy Spirit, teaching them to observe all I have commanded you. And behold, I am with you all days to the end of time.

[44] Mark 16:15–16: Go out to the whole world and preach the gospel to every creature. Whoever believes and is baptised will be saved. Whoever refuses to believe will be condemned.

[45] Matthew 24:14: This gospel of the kingdom will be preached to the whole world, as testimony to all nations. Then will come the end.

[46] Joel 2:28–9: (also Acts 2:17–18) It will come to pass that I will pour out my spirit on all flesh. Your sons and your daughters shall prophesy. Your old men shall dream dreams and your young men shall see visions. Moreover, upon my servants, men and women, in those days I will pour forth my spirit.

[47] Hosea 2:23–4: I will have mercy on her that was without mercy. I will say to that which was not my people: You are my people.

[48] Hosea 1:10: Where it was said to them: you are not my people; it shall be said to them: You are children of the living God.

⁴⁹ Romans 7:24: Who will rescue me from the body of this death?

⁵⁰ John 14:12: Whoever believes in me will perform the same works as I do myself, and will do even greater things.

⁵¹ Proverbs 10:1: A wise son makes his father glad.

⁵² Romans 2:24: Through you, the name of the Lord is blasphemed among the nations.

⁵³ 1 Samuel 12:3: Tell me: whose ox have I taken? I will return it.

⁵⁴ 2 Corinthians 12:15: I most gladly will spend and be spent myself for your souls.

⁵⁵ Galatians 1:20: The things I write to you: behold, before God, I do not lie.

⁵⁶ 2 Corinthians 8:9: Our Lord Jesus Christ became poor for your sake.

⁵⁷ Psalm 54(55):23: Cast your care upon the Lord and he will sustain you.

⁵⁸ 1 Peter 4:19: Cast your souls in good deeds to the faithful creator.

⁵⁹ 2 Corinthians 5:20: We are ambassadors for Christ.

⁶⁰ Psalm 116 (114–15):12: What return can I make to the Lord for his generosity to me?

⁶¹ Matthew 20:22: Can you drink the cup I am going to drink? Matthew 26:39: If possible, let this cup pass.

⁶² Romans 8:16,17: We are children of God and heirs also: heirs of God and co-heirs with Christ.

⁶³ 1 John 2:17: The world is passing away; but the one who does the will of God abides forever.

NOTES ON
THE *CONFESSIO*

There are many translations of the writings of St Patrick available. This translation is offered so as to make one easily available at a low cost, in order to encourage familiarity with the writings.

★

Exact dates for St Patrick are uncertain. His arrival in Ireland is often dated as 432, and his death as occurring in 461.

★

Printing did not come until hundreds of years later. Our copies of the writings of Patrick are in 'man-uscript' – hand-written. There are eight manuscripts in existence. The oldest (A.D. 807) is in the *Book of Armagh* in Trinity College, Dublin.

★

Nowadays, we usually think of a 'confession' as when a person acknowledges some guilt for wrongdoing. An older use has other meanings:

Confession of sin.
Confession of God's greatness—Praise.
Confession of Faith—as in the Creed, a profession of faith.

The Confession of St Patrick is mostly the second usage: the telling of the greatness of God as Patrick has experienced it in his own life, despite all his limitations. There is some of the third usage (as in *section 4* of the Confession), and a little of the first (*sections 26* and *27*).

★

Patrick often quotes parts of the Bible directly. Even more frequently he uses phrases from the Bible as a normal part of his writing. Some of the more obvious quotations are annotated in the endnotes. To give every single possible allusion would make this translation far too unwieldy. Thomas O'Loughlin and Daniel Conneely (see bibliography) offer more than 500 references.

NOTES ON
REFERENCES
TO BOOKS
OF THE BIBLE

Which Bible did Patrick use? The different parts of the Bible which we call the 'Books of the Bible' were written in Hebrew and in Greek over a very long period of time. Some passages existed in spoken form and were passed on by word of mouth from one generation to the next, before being written down. The work of translating the Bible into the everyday language of people has been going on for a long time. Before the time of Jesus Christ, the Hebrew writings had been translated into Greek for Jews who grew up where that was the language. Today, there are many different translations of the Bible into some languages, such as English; some other languages have as yet no translation, or an incomplete one. St Jerome, who died when Patrick was a young man, worked on a new translation into Latin (we call it the 'Vulgate'). There are detailed studies of the sources of the Scripture Patrick used, and of various other writings with which he seems to have been familiar. See Conneely and O'Loughlin.

★

In Patrick's time, the books of the Bible had not yet been divided into chapters and verse numbers, as we use nowadays. Manuscripts could be written without even spaces between words and sentences, and without punctuation. The chapters and verses are not original. There were some divisions used at times; but the system of chapters generally in use today was devised in 1205 by Stephen Langton, a professor in Paris, later Archbishop of Canterbury, who put them into a Vulgate edition of the Bible. Robert Stephanus, a book printer in Paris, is credited with our division of the chapters into verses in 1551.

★

The references to the Bible given in this booklet follow the divisions into chapters and verses we use nowadays, so you can look them up in your own Bible to get a feel for the context of the pieces he uses. In your Bible, you'll find a list of the contents – what we call the different 'books' of the Bible, even though they were not written as 'books' as we use the word today. The first number after the name of the book is the chapter number. The next number(s) give the verse numbers—this is a way of numbering the sentences or parts of sentences in each chapter, so that it's easy to find the place. For example, the first reference given in the Confession is Daniel 9:4–6. This is the Book of Daniel, chapter 9, verses 4 to 6.

★

Depending on the Bible you follow, you may find references to Books which you cannot find in your Bible. Check whether you have the full Christian Bible, or just what we call the 'Old Testament' or the 'New Testament'. Even if you have both, you may still find references to Books not in your Bible. In this translation, there is reference to the Book of Tobit, to the Book of Sirach (also called Ecclesiasticus) and to the Book of Wisdom. These are books accepted as the inspired Word of God by some Christian churches, and not by others. These are often called the 'Apocrypha' or the 'Deuterocanonical' Books.

★

Where a Psalm is referred to, numbering of Psalms varies. There are 150 Psalms in all Bibles, but some combine two where another translation numbers them separately. If you can't find the reference, look at a Psalm one or two before or after the number given, and you should find what you want. Verse numbers can also vary a little.

BIBLIOGRAPHY

Bieler, Ludwig 1952 *Libri Epistolorum Sancti Patricii Episcopi*, Irish Manuscripts Commission, Dublin (a study of the Latin texts in the manuscripts).

Conneely, Daniel 1993 *The Letters of St Patrick*, An Sagart, An Daingean (a study of the sources of the *Confessio*. Latin, with Irish and English translations).

de Paor, Máire 1998 *Patrick: the Pilgrim Apostle of Ireland*, Veritas, Dublin (a study of the literary form. Latin, with English translation).

de Paor, Liam 1993 *St Patrick's World*, Four Courts Press, Dublin (English translation, and many other documents).

Duffy, Joseph 1975 *Patrick in his own words*, Veritas, Dublin (Latin, with English translation).

Johnston, Alfred 1997 *St Patrick's Spiritual Pilgrimage*, Tentmaker Print, Stoke-on-Trent (English translation).

Mac Philbin, Liam 1961 *Mise Pádraig*, FÁS (Latin, with Irish translation).

O'Loughlin, Thomas 1999 *St Patrick: The Man and his Works*, Triangle, London (English translation).